ANIMALS ATTACK!

Killer Bees

Toney Allman

KH

KIDHAVEN
PRESS™

THOMSON
————✦————™
GALE

San Diego • Detroit • New York • San Francisco • Cleveland
New Haven, Conn. • Waterville, Maine • London • Munich

THOMSON

———✷———™

GALE

© 2004 by KidHaven Press. KidHaven Press is an imprint of The Gale Group, Inc., a division of Thomson Learning, Inc.

KidHaven™ and Thomson Learning™ are trademarks used herein under license.

For more information, contact
KidHaven Press
27500 Drake Rd.
Farmington Hills, MI 48331-3535
Or you can visit our Internet site at http://www.gale.com

LIBRARY OF CONGRESS CATALOGING-IN-PUBLICATION DATA
Allman, Toney.
Killer Bees / by Toney Allman.
p. cm.—(Animals attack)
Summary: Describes killer bees.
Includes bibliographical references and index.
ISBN 0-7377-1541-3 (hardback : alk. paper)
1. Killer bees—United States—Juvenile literature. 2. Killer bees—United States—Juvenile literature. [1. Killer bees. 2. Killer bee attacks.] I. Title. II. Series.
2004
597.98'4—dc22
2003

Printed in the United States of America

Contents

Chapter 1
Aggressive Killer Bees   4

Chapter 2
Frightening and Painful Attacks   14

Chapter 3
Almost Deadly Attacks   22

Chapter 4
Bee Experts   31

Notes   40

Glossary   42

For Further Exploration   43

Index   45

Picture Credits   47

About the Author   48

Aggressive
Killer Bees

One small honeybee, buzzing around a flower, does not look like much of a threat. Even if a bee stings, it usually causes only temporary pain and swelling. Dozens, hundreds, sometimes thousands– of attacking bees, however, are an entirely different story. This dangerous mass attack is the behavior of the terrifying honeybees known as killer bees. With amazing accuracy, a swarming mass of these killer honeybees will dive toward its victim's head, drawn by the moisture of eyes, nose, mouth, and ears. Relentlessly each bee plunges its **stinger** into whatever bit of skin it can reach. As the stinger is driven in, the bee's poison, or **venom**, is released. Unless the victim can escape the mass attack, enough poison can be injected into his or her body to cause death.

The Stinger

The honeybee has a stinger on the rear of its **abdomen** from which it releases venom to attack its enemy. The stinger is like a sharp little spear with

Killer bees are very aggressive, attacking their victims as an angry swarm.

barbed hooks on it. The venom inside the stinger is released whenever the bee stings a victim.

The killer bee, like all honeybees, sacrifices its life when it stings. The stinger is driven deep into the victim's flesh and is held there by the barbs. When the bee withdraws, the stinger and much of the bee's abdomen are torn away. Each killer bee can sting only once, and then it dies.

Bees with Attitude

In most ways, killer bees live and act the way ordinary honeybees do. They sting only to protect themselves or their homes. They live together in **colonies** of thousands of individuals, in homes called **hives**. They make honey and store it for food. They have guard bees that protect the hive and warn of any threat.

Killer bees are different from ordinary honeybees in their defensive and aggressive behavior. The ordinary bees in Europe and in North and South America are called European honeybees. European honeybees are gentle. They are slow to anger, have only a few guard bees in the hive, and will give up an attack quickly when the enemy runs away. It is unusual for them to mount a mass attack because they are so good-tempered and calm.

Killer bees, however, are nervous and irritable around the hive. Unlike European honeybees, killer bees have many guard bees and are quick to sting. Killer bees carry no more venom than other bees,

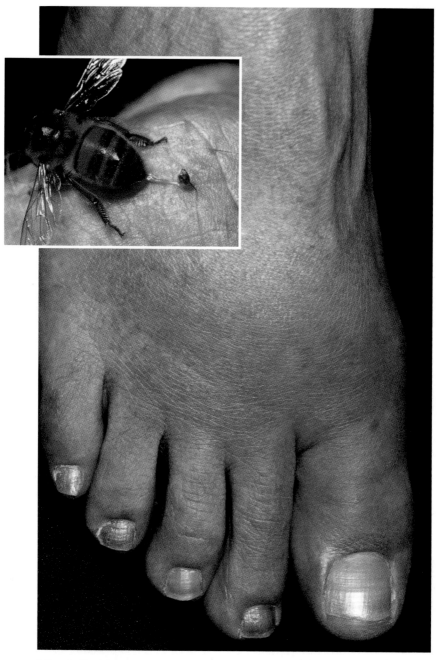

The killer bee uses its spear-like stinger (inset) to inject venom into its victim. Here a person's foot is swollen after being stung.

but they are likely to attack in large numbers. They will attack fiercely and by the thousands, often with no warning.

African Honeybees

Killer bees originated in Africa and are also called African honeybees. In Africa the honeybees' extra aggressiveness helps them to survive. They build their hives almost anywhere, often close to the

Honeybees swarm around their treetop hive. Killer bees viciously attack any animal that comes too close to their hive.

ground, where people or animals may stumble upon them by accident. In the wild they are usually found in trees, piles of brush, rotting logs, or under rock piles. African honeybees may also build hives in house walls, sheds, water meters, abandoned appliances, or under manhole covers.

Defending the Hive

African honeybees will fight angrily to defend their hive against the many **predators** that would like to steal the hive's honey or eat their young. When a predator comes too near the hive, guard bees instantly react. They release a special chemical called a **pheromone**, which all the other bees can smell. The pheromone tells the whole hive to come out ready to attack and sting! Within seconds any animal or person near the hive is driven off by a fierce, determined attack. Even elephants will run from the painful mass attack of African honeybees.

People who live in Africa know how aggressive African honeybees can be. They are very careful not to disturb the bees' homes. They know to run quickly if an angry bee is checking them out. When people are around a hive, they move extremely slowly and quietly so as not to alert the bees. Even so, many people are painfully stung each year in swarming attacks. A few people are killed when they are caught by surprise.

People in countries outside of Africa have little experience coping with the aggressive African honeybee. So when the African honeybee was accidentally released in South America, few people were prepared to cope with the danger.

Coming to America

In 1956 a scientist in Brazil was studying African honeybees in his laboratory. Some of these bees escaped, bred with the European honeybees in Brazil, and started new colonies of Africanized honeybees. These bees were so aggressive that they took over almost all the wild honeybees' hives. Their colonies grew so well and so rapidly that the bees began spreading into other countries throughout South America. By 1990 the Africanized honeybees had reached North America and proceeded to colonize Arizona, Nevada, Texas, Colorado, and California.

By 1990, killer bees had colonized European honeybee hives in North America.

Killer bees look just like European honeybees, so people were unprepared for relentless, aggressive behavior when they saw a beehive. People who had never seen Africanized honeybees suddenly found themselves viciously attacked by swarms of angry bees. In the years since 1956, more than one thousand people have been killed by Africanized honeybees in South and North America. Many more have been hospitalized with dangerous illnesses caused by the bees' venom. In the Americas these new threatening creatures were nicknamed "killer bees."

When Killer Bees Attack

Even though death from a killer bee attack is rare, painful encounters are becoming common as killer bees spread. In the United States, people usually disturb a colony of killer bees by mistake. The noise of a lawn mower close to a brush pile, the smack of a ball against a hollow tree, the opening of a door on an old abandoned car–all may disturb a killer bee hive. Any noise or movement close to the hive is treated as a threat to their colony by the touchy bees. Even thunder may anger them. Killer bees can stay angry for days after they have been disturbed. So a quiet passerby may still be seen as an enemy and be attacked.

The bees swarm out of the hive, ready to do battle with the intruder. People and pets, such as dogs, horses, and cats, can suddenly find themselves under attack. The bees swarm first toward the head of their victim. If enough bees live in the colony, they can

Built to Attack!

Two sets of wings beat one hundred eighty times a second, and allow the bee to fly as fast as twenty-two miles per hour.

Compound eyes sense light and movement.

The bee's six legs have tiny claws that help the bee hold onto its victim during an attack.

Sharp, barbed stinger releases venom into the bee's victim. Each bee can sting only one time.

cover the body of the victim completely. Running away is difficult. Killer bees will chase their enemies for up to a mile before giving up. Jumping into a pool or pond does not help either. The angry bees wait, hovering above the water until the victim comes up for air, and then sting again. Rescuers are also in danger. Angry killer bees will attack them, too. The bees attack anything that moves and never give up. Many animals are killed, but most people are able to escape to a building, house, or car to save themselves.

Here to Stay

Luckily people usually can survive even hundreds of bee stings with medical help. People in the Americas are also learning how to behave around these aggressive killer bees. As Africanized honeybees become a permanent part of the American environment, people have to learn to live with this new kind of bee.

Chapter 1

Frightening and Painful Attacks

When killer bees first move into an area, people are unprepared for their aggressive behavior. People assume that the bees they see are gentle honeybees. They think they can scare off the bees or swat them or share a yard with them, just as they have always done with bees. These assumptions can cause trouble.

A Neighborhood Attacked

In the town of Bisbee, Arizona, a killer bee attack surprised everyone. It was a warm summer morning in early August 1998 when Carmen Chavez noticed some bees flying around inside his warehouse. He tried to scare the bees away by spraying bug spray at the entrance to their hive. He did not know that this was no ordinary beehive. Eighty thousand killer bees lived inside.

The killer bees came shooting out of the hive, looking for enemies to attack. Within minutes, they were swarming through the whole neighborhood and stinging any person or animal they found. Two dogs were attacked and stung. People outside found themselves attacked with no warning. Cars driving down the street were attacked. Two people driving a truck stopped in the middle of the street and ran away as the bees swarmed them. Debrah Strait, who

Killer bees terrorized the residents of the small town of Bisbee, Arizona, in 1998.

lived in the neighborhood, was driving her car down the street when she found her way blocked by the stopped, empty truck. Unfortunately her car window was half open. The bees swarmed inside to attack her.

Fleeing the Swarm

Strait tried to wave the bees back out the window, but they kept coming into her car. Quickly she parked and leaped out of the car. Then she tried to escape by running away as fast as she could. She fled the street and headed toward the home of a neighbor, Cleone Gerkin. The bees surrounded and followed her. Strait said, "I was screaming mostly for help, but I couldn't see anybody, I

Although killer bees (inset) look just like European honey-bees (below), they are much more aggressive.

couldn't hear anybody, and I knew I needed somehow to get out of the swarm."[1]

When Strait arrived in her neighbor's yard, she was covered in bees and was frantically ripping at her clothing. Cleone Gerkin was seventy-five years old, but she bravely tried to help. Together the two women used a garden hose to wash off the bees and get Debrah inside. Gerkin said later, "I was so frightened; the bees were just swarming around her. Her hair was literally covered with bees. She had taken her shirt off, and her back and her chest were covered, too."[2]

While Strait was fighting to escape, other people were being stung. Fifteen people were stung that day, including a police officer, David Gonzales, who was stung many times as he tried to help the neighborhood victims.

To the Rescue

Firefighters who rushed to the neighborhood sprayed a soapy-water foam on all the bees they could reach. Soap suffocates bees. They breathe through their abdomens, and the soapy foam blocks their airholes. Many bees were killed, but many others flew angrily around the neighborhood for hours, searching for more enemies to attack. The police had to block off the neighborhood and close down the streets until an expert bee handler could destroy the rest of the bees.

Along with seven other people, Debrah Strait was taken to the hospital. She had been stung more than two hundred times. There were bee stings even inside her ear. Strait did not suffer any lasting harm from her terrible experience. With medical help she completely recovered, as did all the victims of the bee attack. The attack would not have happened if Chavez had not tried to scare off the killer bees by himself. The people of Bisbee learned that only expert bee handlers can get rid of bees safely.

A Home Attacked

Sometimes killer bees will attack just because a person comes too close to their hive. This is what happened to Jim and Becky Brantley in the summer of 2002.

The Brantleys lived in Texas, where they had a backyard garden. A hive of honeybees had lived in their garden for five years and never bothered anyone. The gentle bees were welcome in the Brantley yard. Then—although the Brantleys did not know it— killer bees took over the hive. One July morning Becky Brantley stepped outside. The bees reacted as if her presence were a threat. She said, "I was sitting on the front porch swing bench when all of a sudden a bee stung me on my head. Then out of nowhere, they were swarming me."[3] She jumped up and ran inside the house. The bees chased her inside, and she called for her husband to help. When Jim Brantley got to her, he found bees everywhere, stinging his wife and attacking their two cats. He tried to kill the bees that were in the house, but there were so many that it took him forty-five minutes before he succeeded. Then he used the telephone to call for emergency help.

A Mass of Bees

When the sheriff arrived at the Brantley house, so many angry bees were swarming he could not get out of his car. Birds flying over the house were being attacked, and the sheriff saw the birds falling out of the sky. For hours the killer bees circled the

A beekeeper removes a hive from a house. Only expert bee handlers can remove bees safely.

house, waiting for someone to move. Jim Brantley said of the bees, "They are like a black mass that tumbles in the sky."[4]

Both Brantleys were fine after the attack, and their cats were unhurt. Now that they know killer bees have taken over the hives in their area, the Brantleys will not let a beehive stay in their garden. Killer bee hives must be kept far away from where people live. Jim Brantley had some advice for others after his frightening experience: "Be on the lookout."[5]

Do Not Disturb!

People need to watch for killer bees, stay far away from their hives, and never disturb them. Theo Flippen, an eighty-eight-year-old man in Nevada, learned that lesson the hard way. "Well, I disturbed them and they didn't like it,"[6] he said. Flippen had bees in the trees in his yard and wanted to get rid of them, so he threw a handful of kitchen cleanser into one tree hole. Furious killer bees streamed out of the hole and attacked him. Flippen took off running with the bees fiercely stinging his head. He fled next door to his neighbor's yard, fell down, then jumped up and ran farther away—out into the street—and fell again. All the time he was fighting the bees. His neighbor called 911 and rescue workers, who took him to the hospital.

Firefighters sprayed the trees in Flippen's yard with foam. They found several hives in the trees and smothered them all, destroying the bees. Flippen was lucky to be able to run away from the bees. At the hospital he

Only experts should destroy killer bee hives.

was found to have been stung only about thirty times. He was medically treated but did not have to stay in the hospital. He said later, "I grabbed a handful of [cleanser and threw] it in that hole and I never should have done it."[7] Flippen learned a painful lesson about disturbing killer bees. Like the people of Bisbee, he found out that only experts should try to destroy a hive.

People who are attacked by killer bees describe the experience as terrifying. Of course, the many stings are painful, too. Killer bees are very good at teaching people to leave their hives alone.

Chapter 3

Almost Deadly Attacks

Sometimes killer bee attacks are so severe that people can be seriously hurt. The people who are in the most danger from mass attacks are the very old, the very young, or people who are already weak or sick. These people cannot fight off the effects of the venom easily and often cannot even run away.

Terror on the Street

One such horrible attack happened to an elderly woman in Nevada in April 2000. Toha Bergerub was a seventy-seven-year-old immigrant to the United States who lived in Las Vegas. One Monday morning she was walking down the street by her home, going to visit her landlord. Suddenly killer bees came boiling out of a hollow tree that stood in a yard about eighty feet away from her. No one knows why the bees attacked a woman who was just walking by, but the bees swarmed over her and quickly covered her body. Terrified, Bergerub tried to swat the bees away. She could not run away, and the more she struck at the bees, the more they stung her. She explained, "I slap, I slap at them, but then there are more. Then more, more, and there are too many. I said 'Why? Why?' They are all over."[8]

Bergerub was frightened, in pain, and thought she was going to die. Within minutes she had fallen to the curb and sat motionless and helpless. "I cannot do

Killer bees can seriously injure their victims. Multiple stings can even be fatal.

anything. I can't hit them. I can't catch them. I can do nothing,"she said.[9]

She knew she was in trouble, but it seemed no one could save her. She said, "I felt pain, real pain, there was too much. But no one could help. No one could do anything. The cars go by, but no one stops because of the bees."[10] She gave up and continued sitting on the curb, enveloped in stinging bees.

Battling the Bees

Bergerub felt alone, but many people saw the terrible attack and tried to help. Witnesses on the street immediately called 911 and reported the emergency. Two

The killer bee's venom causes painful swelling and breathing problems.

police officers rushed to the scene, dashed out of their cars, and tried to reach Bergerub. Angry killer bees attacked the police officers so badly they were forced to run back to the safety of their cars and watch helplessly as Bergerub, covered in bees, got weaker.

Then firefighters and the rescue squad arrived. The firefighters were dressed in protective clothing, with special shields over their heads. They were able to get close enough to Bergerub to spray over her head with water from their fire hose. The heavy spray of water distracted the bees enough so that the firefighters were able to pick up their patient and get her away from the bees. Then Bergerub was taken to the hospital.

Saving a Life

The attack was over, but the danger was not. At the hospital, doctors discovered that Bergerub had been stung more than five hundred times. The stingers were embedded so heavily in her skin that her face appeared to be growing a prickly beard.

Doctors had to carefully remove each stinger. They used tweezers to pluck out some stingers. Then they gently scraped off others with a plastic card and lifted still more out with sticky adhesive tape. Doctors gave Bergerub oxygen to help her breathe, as well as giving her medicines, which included an **antihistamine**. Antihistamines help people fight off the effects of venom by preventing swelling and breathing problems. They also gave her medicine to help

Killer bees attack a beekeeper as he checks their hive.

lessen the severe pain of the many stings. The frail, elderly woman was placed in intensive care. She had been stung so much and had received so much venom that the doctors were afraid she would not live. Doctors call what happened to her "high venom load." The venom load in her body was equal to the amount of two rattlesnake bites.

Tougher than the Bees

By Tuesday morning, however, Bergerub surprised everyone with her improvement. She was tougher than anyone thought. She recovered rapidly from her terrible experience and, after four days, was even able to talk to newspaper reporters about her ordeal. Although her face and body were still swollen and blotchy from the stings, she said the pain was much better and she was ready to go home. After seven days she was released from the hospital as strong and healthy as she had ever been.

The killer bees that attacked Bergerub were destroyed, as was their hive. The property owner cut down the "bee tree" so that no other bees could use it for a home. Bergerub developed a real fear of bees

After an attack, killer bees must be destroyed to prevent further attacks.

after her attack, but she also felt very grateful toward the firefighters and doctors who saved her life. She said, "I will write them a letter, and I will talk to them. I always do that, write a letter, to anyone who helps me. My mother always said you have to do good for people who help you."[11]

People, like Bergerub, who suffer mass attacks, almost always need doctors and rescue workers in order to survive. Sometimes, though, aid can come from unexpected places.

A Swift and Massive Attack

In Guadalupe, Texas, A.C. Gembler was rescued by two strangers when he suffered a mass attack by killer bees. It was late summer 2002 and Gembler was mowing his grass when he accidentally disturbed a hive of killer bees. Perhaps the noise of the lawn mower upset the bees. Or perhaps his mower bumped into their hive. Gembler did not remember. The bees poured out of the hive and attacked so fast that Gembler was quickly overcome. "It was just a horrible feeling because they just covered my face,"[12] he said. He was a heavy man, weighing three hundred pounds, and was unable to run away. Within minutes Gembler was lying on the ground, unconscious and covered in stinging bees.

The Good Samaritans

Two men who were driving by saw Gembler on the ground and engulfed in swarming bees. With great

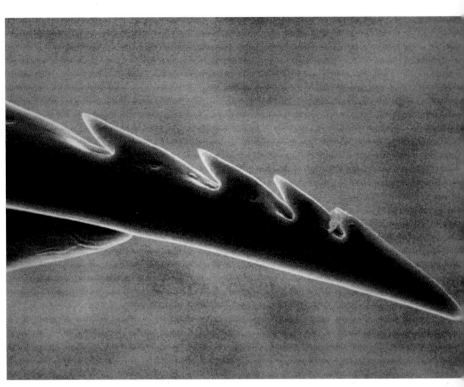

Backward-pointing barbs make the killer bee's stinger very difficult to remove from its victim.

bravery the strangers stopped, forced their way to the victim's body, grabbed him, and threw him in the back of their truck. Then they drove him to a nearby fire station where an ambulance took him to the hospital. "Boy, I tell you," he said later, "that was a real blessing."[13]

Four Hundred Stings

At the hospital, doctors discovered that Gembler had been stung more than four hundred times. Stingers were pulled from every part of his body, including his tongue. "They even got in my mouth,

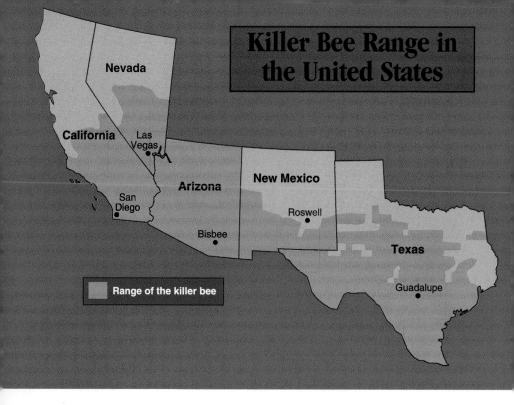

Killer Bee Range in the United States

Nevada

California
Las Vegas

San Diego

Arizona

Bisbee

New Mexico

Roswell

Texas

Guadalupe

Range of the killer bee

my nose," said Gembler. The doctors even had to pull two live bees out of his ear. Gembler was strong enough to need to stay in the hospital only three days, but he knew he could not have survived without the help of the doctors, firefighters, and his two rescuers. He was very thankful to the two strangers who had saved him. In the hospital he said, "If they wouldn't have risked their self for me, I wouldn't be here. I wouldn't be ready to go home."[14]

Killer bees are the most dangerous when hundreds of bees sting in a mass attack. When that happens, the help of firefighters, police officers, rescue squads, hospitals, and even private citizens may be needed to save a life.

Chapter 4

Bee Experts

Killer bees are dangerous. As colonies continue to spread, experts on honeybees have been researching the Africanized variety. These experts' experiences help everyone know more about what to do when he or she sees a beehive or becomes a victim of a bee attack.

A Beekeeper Investigates

Sue Hubbell was a **beekeeper** with many years experience raising European honeybees. She raised bees for their honey and to **pollinate** crops. Her bees lived in specially built hives, with removable frames inside for storing honey. In 1991, before killer bees had

A beekeeper protects himself with a bee suit and smoke as he checks a hive.

reached the United States, Hubbell decided to learn more about them and how much trouble they might cause. She traveled to Guatemala, where killer bees had taken over hives, so she could see for herself.

 Killer Bees

Many Guatemalan beekeepers told Hubbell the bees were not killers. The beekeepers raised them for their honey and were not afraid. Other beekeepers told her the bees were vicious. They told stories of bees killing farm animals and even a village baby.

When Hubbell visited beekeeper Jorge Mansilla, she saw how successful Guatemalan beekeepers had adjusted to killer bees. Before the killer bees came, beekeepers used to keep beehives right beside their houses. That was why animals and children were attacked when the killer bees arrived. Mansilla's beehives were far away from where people lived.

Bee Suits and Smokers

Beekeepers in Guatemala also learned to wear coveralls, gloves, and veils when they worked with their hives. Hubbell and Mansilla visited his hives, wearing bee suits and carrying a big bee smoker. The bee smoker puffs harmless smoke that quiets bees, making them slow to anger. As Mansilla smoked his bees, Hubbell opened some hives, lifting out frames to check the bees as she would at home. She said, "As we worked on down the row of hives, more and more bees flew up into the air as bees from each successive hive egged one another on into a display of defensive behavior. *Plok! Plok!* They began to throw themselves against our veils."[15] Still, neither Hubbell nor Mansilla were stung. The smoke and clothing protected them.

Hubbell believed the United States could adjust to the presence of killer bees. She learned in Guatemala that "they must be kept on individual stands well away from animals and houses, and their keepers have learned to wear protective clothing and carry jumbo-sized bee smokers."[16]

Not Always Dangerous

In some ways, Hubbell saw that killer bees were no different from European honeybees. She said, "Any bee, even a killer bee, will not sting while happily collecting pollen or nectar unless she is stepped on or otherwise attacked. She can only sting once and dies afterward, so she will reserve that suicidal gesture for the defense of her home—her hive, its honey, and her sister bees."[17] No one has to be afraid of the sight of a bee. Only approaching a hive is dangerous.

A honeybee's head magnified many times its normal size shows in detail the bee's eyes, antennae, hair, and mouthparts.

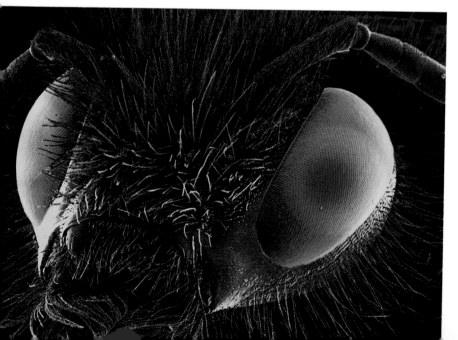

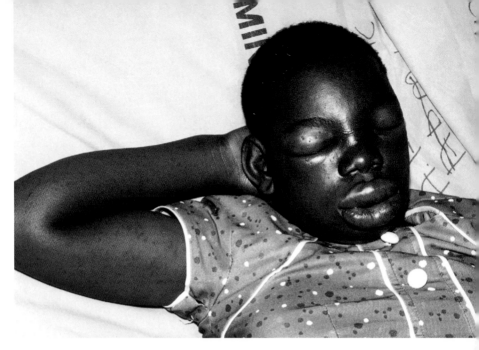

This woman's lips and eyelids are painfully swollen after bees stung her.

Beekeepers in the United States learned to adjust when killer bees invaded their hives, too. They found that working with killer bees was not easy, but it could be done.

Killer Bee Honey

Reed Booth was a beekeeper and bee **exterminator** in Arizona. He not only kept hives of killer bees and sold the honey, but also removed and destroyed hives that were a threat to people. When he had gentle European honeybees, Booth kept his hives close to his house. He could harvest his honey easily, brush the bees out of his way, and then walk away when his job was done. Things changed once killer bees were in his hives.

No Fun

Booth moved his beehives far away from any house. He drove to them in his van and dressed in protective clothing. He hurried to harvest his honey from the bee frames, rushed back to his van with the honey, and drove away as fast as possible. After about a mile, the angry bees stopped chasing his van, and he could safely drive home. "Bee-keeping used to be a lot of fun," Booth said, "but not anymore. When I get within 20 feet of the hives, it feels like hail hitting my suit. I can smell the venom dripping from their stingers."[18]

When he talked about killer bees, Booth said, "They are mean," but he was not afraid to work with them. He was the beekeeper who destroyed the bees that attacked Debrah Strait in Bisbee. Bee-keepers know how to destroy a beehive safely. They often work after sunset when bees are slow and cannot see well. They use smokers, protective clothing, soap foam, or poison, if necessary. People can call on experts like Booth if they see a beehive in their area. Sometimes Booth would destroy the bees, but sometimes he collected the bees and brought them back to his hives to make honey for him. He joked, "I get paid to remove swarms, so I take the money and the honey."[19]

They Are Here; They Are Mean

Beekeepers have learned how to handle their killer bees, but no one can stop wild killer bees from

An Africanized honeybee buzzes above a flower. Killer bees have taken over European honeybee hives in much of the southwestern United States.

showing up wherever they want. Bee experts worry about keeping track of where killer bees live and protecting the public from them. Sometimes the experts have trouble protecting themselves from attack.

Gerald Loper was a bee researcher in Arizona who discovered that even a veil was not enough protection. In June 1998 Loper decided to check on a wild killer bee hive in some cliffs. He was wearing a bee suit, gloves, and a veil. When he got close to the hive, bees boiled out and attacked him. The bees were so determined and fierce that they stung through the bee suit and veil. Loper had to run away. He was stung more than one hundred times before he could escape.

In September Loper returned to the cliffs, but this time he wore a clear, hard helmet to shield his head, along with his other protective clothing. He walked up to the hive quietly, but in less than a minute the angry bees swarmed him by the thousands. They smacked against his helmet and fought to get through his suit. "This is the worst-case scenario we were talking about 20 years ago," he said. "People would go to Brazil to see these bad bees and say, 'We don't want them up here.' Well, they're here."[20]

Expert Advice

Researchers, like Loper, cannot stop the killer bees from colonizing in America, but they can track the bees and warn communities of where they are. Firefighters and police can wear shields and protective clothing, as the experts do, when they try to

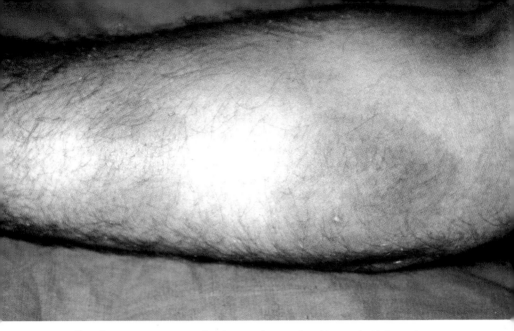

Killer bees can attack through protective clothing, leaving painful stings like these.

save a victim from attack. Hives that threaten people can be destroyed by experts.

Experts warn that no one should go near or bother a beehive. People should never swat at bees, either. When bees are slapped, they release pheromones which call more bees to the attack. A hive should be removed only by an expert exterminator.

Run and Take Cover

If killer bees attack, people should cover their heads and run quickly toward the nearest building or car. Even if some bees follow, it is still better to be inside. Since each bee can sting only once, dozens of bees inside are safer than thousands attacking outside. Everyone should learn what to do if killer bees attack because killer bees are here to stay.

Notes

Chapter 2: Frightening and Painful Attacks

1. Quoted in Ignacio Ibarra and Jim Erickson, "The Panic, the Fear," *Arizona Daily Star*, August 5, 1998. www.stingshield.com.
2. Quoted in Ibarra and Erickson, "The Panic, the Fear."
3. Quoted in Dave Cadriel, *Alpine Avalanche,* October 30, 2003. www.stingshield.com.
4. Quoted in Cadriel, *Alpine Avalanche.*
5. Quoted in Cadriel, *Alpine Avalanche.*
6. Quoted in Yetta Gibson, KLAS-TV Las Vegas, May 15, 2003. www.stingshield.com.
7. Quoted in Yetta Gibson, KLAS-TV Las Vegas.

Chapter 3: Almost Deadly Attacks

8. Quoted in Glenn Puit, "Sting Victim Feared Death from Attack," *Las Vegas Review-Journal,* April 1, 2000. www.stingshield.com.
9. Quoted in Puit, "Sting Victim Feared Death from Attack."
10. Quoted in Puit, "Sting Victim Feared Death from Attack."
11. Quoted in Puit, "Sting Victim Feared Death from Attack."
12. Quoted in KSAT-TV 12 San Antonio, September 19, 2002. www.stingshield.com.

13. Quoted in KSAT-TV 12 San Antonio.
14. Quoted in KSAT-TV 12 San Antonio.

Chapter 4: Bee Experts

15. Sue Hubbell, *Broadsides from the Other Orders: A Book of Bugs*. New York: Random House, 1993. p. 101
16. Hubbell, *Broadsides from the Other Orders*.
17. Hubbell, *Broadsides from the Other Orders*.
18. Quoted in Jerry Fink, "Killer Bees Make Honey to Die For," *Las Vegas Sun*, May 15, 2000.
19. Quoted in Fink, "Killer Bees Make Honey to Die For."
20. Quoted in Associated Press, "'Worst Case' Bees in Arizona," *CFZ Newsfiles*, September 22, 1998. http://cfzarchive.tripod.com.

Glossary

abdomen: The rear part of the honeybee body where the stinger is attached. The bee not only digests food but also breathes with its abdomen.

antihistamine: A drug used to ease an allergic reaction to venoms.

beekeeper: A person who keeps, cares for, and raises bees.

colony: A community of thousands of bees, consisting of one queen, many worker and guard bees, and drones.

exterminator: A person who removes or destroys dangerous insects or other pests.

hive: A bee colony's home.

pheromone: A chemical produced by a bee that stimulates other bees to respond to a threat.

pollinate: To fertilize a flowering plant by spreading the pollen in the blossoms from flower to flower. Then the plant can make seeds from which new plants can grow.

predator: An animal that lives by hunting other animals.

stinger: The slender, spearlike barbed organ at the tip of a bee's abdomen that stings and injects venom into an enemy.

venom: Poison released by the bee when it stings a victim.

For Further Exploration

Books

George S. Fichter, *Bees, Wasps, and Ants*. Racine, Wisconsin: Western, (New York: Golden Book), 1993. Learn the difference among different kinds of bees, bumblebees, and wasps.

Charles Micucci, *The Life and Times of the Honey Bee*. New York: Ticknor & Fields Books for Young Readers, 1995. This easy-to-read book is chock-full of interesting honeybee facts. It describes the life cycle of bees, the makeup of the hive, the honeybee dance, and much more.

Laurence Pringle, *Here Come the Killer Bees*. New York: William Morrow, 1986. This book offers an interesting history of the killer bees, along with stories of bee/human interactions and ways to stay safe.

Internet Resources

PBS Online, *Nature*, **"Alien Empire," Bees** www.pbs.org/wnet/nature/alienempire/multimedia/bee.html. See very clear graphics of the body of a honeybee. Click on the body parts for definitions.

Professional Pest Control, "Creature of the Month," African Killer Bees, November 2002. www.no-pest.com/KillerBees.htm. Listen to an audio of a swarm of active bees and see a map of the range of killer bees, as well as many close-up killer bee photographs.

Websites

The Amazing Beecam (http://gears.tucson.ars.ag. gov/beecam/index.html). See a honeybee hive "almost live," and a beekeeper dressing in his bee suit.

Carl Hayden Bee Research Center (http://gears.tucson. ars.ag.gov). Click on the Africanized honeybee page and learn what to do if you are attacked by killer bees or see killer bees around your home.

Draper's Super Bee Apiaries Bee Cam (www. draperbee. com/webcam/beecam.htm). The camera is turned on inside the beehive all the time, and the pictures reload every fifteen seconds. Watch the bees in action.

Honey.Com Just for Kids (www.honey.com/kids/ index.html). Find out interesting facts about the lives of honeybees. Learn how honeybees help the environment and people. Play fun honeybee games.

Index

African honeybees,
8–9
Africanized honeybees,
10, 11, 13, 37
antihistamines, 25–26
attacks
on animals, 11–12, 13
on birds, 19
causes of, 9, 11, 28
on people, 4, 11–13, 22
preventing, 33–34, 36,
39
treatment for, 25–26
see also specific people

beekeepers, 31, 33–36
Bergerub, Toha
attack on, 22–25
treatment of, 25–28
Bisbee, Arizona, 14–18,
36
Booth, Reed, 35–36
Brantley, Jim and Becky,
18–20
Brazil, 10
breathing, 17

characteristics, 6, 8, 11,
12–13, 33
Chavez, Carmen, 14–15,
18
colonies, 6

deaths
of honeybees, 6
of people, 9, 11
defenses, 25

European honeybees, 6,
10

Flippen, Theo, 20–21

Gembler, A.C.,
28–30
Gerkin, Cleone, 16–17
Gonzales, David, 17
Guadalupe, Texas, 28–30
guard bees, 6
Guatemala, 32–33

high venom load, 26
hives

defending, 6, 9, 11
destroying, 36
takeover of, 10
honey, 6
Hubbell, Sue,
    31–34

Loper, Gerald, 38

Mansilla, Jorge, 33

nickname, 11
North America, 11

pheromones, 9, 39
protective clothing, 25,

33, 34, 38

range, 10

smokers, 33
soap, 17
South America, 10, 11,
    32–33
spread, 10
stinger, 4, 5–6
Strait, Debrah, 15–17, 18,
    36

venom
    release of, 4–6
    treatment for, 25–26

Picture Credits

Cover: © Darwin Dale/Photo Researchers, Inc.
© Dr. M. A. Ansary/Photo Researchers, Inc., 35
AP/Wide World Photos, 19, 21, 26
© Art Today, Inc., 10, 12 (bee), 16 (both)
© Anthony Bannister; Gallo Images/CORBIS, 23
© Tom Bean/CORBIS, 15
© Dr. Jeremy Burgess/ Photo Researchers, Inc., 7
  (inset)
© Scott Camazine/ Photo Researchers, Inc., 24
© COREL Corporation, 27
© Darwin Dale/Photo Researchers, Inc., 37
© Dr. Gary Gaugler/Visuals Unlimited, 12 (inset)
© Dr. Ken Greer/Visuals Unlimited, 39
© Bryan Knox; Papilio/CORBIS, 8
© Dr. P. Marazzi/Photo Researchers, Inc., 7
© Michael Pole/CORBIS, 32
© Science Photo Library/Photo Researchers, Inc., 34
© Andrew Syred/Photo Researchers, Inc., 29
© Texas Cooperative Extension, 27 (inset)
© Jim Zuckerman/CORBIS, 5

About the Author

Toney Allman holds degrees from Ohio State University and the University of Hawaii. She currently lives in Virginia. She likes gardening and wild bees, but then, killer bees do not yet live in her state.